Living Word BIBLE STUDIES

NEHEMIAH

Rebuilt and Rebuilding

KATHLEEN BUSWELL NIELSON

P U B L I S H I N G
P.O. BOX 817 • PHILLIPSBURG • NEW JERSEY 08865-0817

Scripture quotations are from *ESV Bible* ® (*The Holy Bible, English Standard Version* ®). Copyright © 2001 by Crossway Bibles, a publishing ministry of Good News Publishers. Used by permission. All rights reserved.

Printed in the United States of America

ISBN: 978-1-59638-372-2

CONTENTS

Contents

FOREWORD

Many Christian congregations in the affluent West have had some exposure to the book of Nehemiah—especially those whose ministries required a capital campaign for building expansion! Yes, unlike some other Old Testament books, many of us have knowledge of Nehemiah, the commendable postexilic Jew who served long ago in Persia at the king's table. We have read of his vocational change to general contractor and of his return to the once proud city of Jerusalem to rebuild its walls.

That said, we should ask, "While we may have read Nehemiah, or heard a series of sermons based on it, have we learned to read it well? Have we heard it on its own terms?" After all, it is one thing to take an Old Testament book into the Christian church; it is quite another to keep it in its original context. Truth be told, Christian studies of a book like Nehemiah often end up bowing to the pressure of using the Bible as a "how-to manual"—a lamentable practice which relegates Nehemiah to a book of mere lessons on leadership, or simply a guidebook for planning successful brick-and-mortar campaigns.

This is where the real strength of Kathleen Nielson's study guide on Nehemiah is seen. As a student of the Scriptures, she refuses to allow us to run roughshod over Nehemiah's original setting, purpose, and intention. We are led into the book as we should be—we are given tools not only to read it, but to read it well.

Christian Bible study guides that make an attempt to bring us into the Hebrew world of divine promises to Abraham and David require great care, and should be written by those who possess an understanding of that world on its own terms. Further, the fruit of their work must demonstrate a mature grasp of biblical theology, so proper connections to Christ and his church can emerge. In Kathleen Nielson, we are blessed to have someone capable of doing both.

I welcome the opportunity to commend her study notes to you. May God remember her, as well as you, for all the good that is done for Christ as a result of time spent reading and listening to this divinely inspired memoir called Nehemiah.

David R. Helm

A PERSONAL WORD
FROM KATHLEEN

I began to write these Bible studies for the women in my own church group at College Church in Wheaton, Illinois. Under the leadership of Kent and Barbara Hughes, the church and that Bible study aimed to proclaim without fail the good news of the Word of God. What a joy, in that study and in many since, to see lives changed by the work of the Word, by the Spirit, for the glory of Christ.

In our Bible study group, we were looking for curriculum that would lead us into the meat of the Word and teach us how to take it in, whole Bible books at a time—the way they are given to us in Scripture. Finally, one of our leaders said, "Kathleen—how about if you just write it!" And so began one of the most joyful projects of my life: the writing of studies intended to help unleash the Word of God in people's lives. The writing began during a busy stage of my life—with three lively young boys and always a couple of college English courses to teach—but through that stage and every busy one since, a serious attention to studying the Bible has helped keep me focused, growing, and alive in the deepest ways. The Word of God will do that. If there's life and power in these studies, it is simply the life and power of the Scriptures to which they point. It is ultimately the life and power of the Savior who shines through all the Scriptures from beginning to end. How we need this life, in the midst of every busy and non-busy stage of our lives!

I don't think it is just the English teacher in me that leads me to this conclusion about our basic problem in Bible study these days: we've forgotten how to *read*! We're so used to fast food that we think we should be able to drive by the Scriptures periodically and pick up some easily digestible truths that someone else has wrapped up neatly for us. We've disowned that process of careful reading . . . observing the words . . . seeing the shape of a book and a passage . . . asking questions that take us into the text rather than away from it . . . digging into the Word and letting it speak! Through such a process, guided by the Spirit, the Word of God truly feeds our souls. Here's my prayer: that, by means of these studies, people would be further enabled to read the Scriptures profitably and thereby find life and nourishment in them, as we are each meant to do.

In all the busy stages of life and writing, I have been continually surrounded by pastors, teachers, and family who encourage and help me in this work, and for that I am grateful. The most wonderful guidance and encouragement come from my husband, Niel, whom I thank and for whom I thank God daily.

May God use these studies to lift up Christ and his Word, for his glory!

INTRODUCTION

Welcome to ten studies in Nehemiah. This Old Testament book tells the dramatic story of God's people led by a godly leader at a crucial point in their history. It was a point of *rebuilding*, after the consequences of sin had devastated the people and their land. The whole biblical story of the Hebrew nation—from the choosing of Abraham, through the Exodus, through the rise and fall of the kingdom—is vital background for the story of Nehemiah. This study, then, begins in Lesson One by putting the story in its biblical context. The unfolding of the book becomes even more beautiful and clear when seen as part of the larger story of God's working to accomplish his covenant promises to his people. Nehemiah is all about a God who preserves his people according to his word—and who calls them to walk in light of that word.

A more specific context for Nehemiah is needed as well. When we look in many Bible versions for introductory notes to Nehemiah, we find simply: "See Ezra." Although the two books were originally separate, many early manuscripts combined them as one story of the Jewish return from exile. Jewish tradition assigns to Ezra the priest the role of compiling and editing the two books, even though the second book is largely made up of Nehemiah's memoirs. Tradition gives Ezra the authorship of Chronicles as well. These books all faithfully chronicle the history of God's people—listing careful genealogies, giving detailed descriptions of religious festivals, keeping close track of the leaders God raised up, and in general offering a picture of a people chosen and preserved by God through generations, for his good purposes. The continuity of this picture is great between Ezra and Nehemiah especially, with Ezra not only perhaps editing both, but also appearing as one of the lead characters in both. The background from Ezra (Lesson Two) directly paves the way for study of the text of Nehemiah, which begins in Lesson Three.

What is to be gained from a study of Nehemiah? This study approaches the text first of all as the inspired Word of God, authoritative and profitable (2 Tim. 3:16–17). God breathed these words through his Spirit into these leaders of Israel centuries ago for the good of God's people both then and now. As we take in these words of Nehemiah, we will certainly notice that we are taking in a good story, with drama, excitement, and a compelling main character. It is amazing to watch Nehemiah the leader through the process of this book—weeping, praying and praying again, planning with godly deliberation, leading with dynamic strength, facing opposition head-on, charting his course unswervingly according to God's Word. Nehemiah can challenge any leader and any *person* who wants to follow God with strength and passion.

Other levels of the story will emerge, however, as we study this book. We will grasp the flow of Old Testament history and the significance of the post-exilic period in that flow. Ezra, Nehemiah, and Esther make up the last part of the Old Testament's historical books, which come in our Bible before the poetic literature and the prophets. We are reading in Nehemiah the final glimpse of God's people mercifully reestablished in Jerusalem after their exile under the Babylonians and before that long, dark, intertestamental period of waiting.

But we will understand not only the human history; we will grasp the divine history as well—for Nehemiah is telling not just the story of the Jewish people. He is telling, above all, the story of *God* at work among his people, accomplishing his sovereign plan to preserve them and bless the nations through them, as he promised Abraham. God's people at this point in history are poor and weak as they reassemble and rebuild Jerusalem and its temple. However, God had promised great things to them and through them, and so they persevere, under godly leaders. As those leaders turn the people's attention to God's Word, it becomes clear (especially to us) that God's promises point to more than an earthly kingdom. The Jews will never again be a magnificent kingdom as in their former days of glory, under David and Solomon. Yet from the Jews will come a promised and glorious king, through whom God will call out a people from all the nations of the earth. This book is about the God who sent his Son—the seed of Abraham—to save his people from their sins. It is about the roots of our salvation in and through the Lord Jesus Christ.

Our method of study, after establishing the context in the first two lessons, will be careful, verse-by-verse, passage-by-passage examination of the text. Historical background and cross-references are provided when they help clarify the text. Several charts will help you read with understanding. Applications will be suggested as they grow out of the story. Our main task will be to look carefully at the words of Nehemiah, to ask questions about those words, to understand them in their immediate and larger contexts, and to learn from them as the people of God. Before each day's work on the lesson, we will do well to pray, asking God for understanding through the power and teaching of his Holy Spirit. We will do well to read and reread the text for that day first, thoughtfully and carefully. The words of the text are beautiful and powerful. May we come away from them, like the people in chapter 8, celebrating with great joy because we have understood the words that were declared to us.

Lesson 1

REBUILDING THE WALLS . . . AGAINST THE BACKGROUND OF THE WHOLE STORY

The book of Nehemiah will amaze us with its dramatic story of rebuilding the walls of Jerusalem. We will enjoy this story even more if we understand its background. Where did these people come from, and who are these families who are struggling to rebuild a broken-down city? These are *God's people*, who show us both *the consequences of disobeying God's law* and *the blessing of receiving God's mercy.*

(Please refer throughout this lesson to the General Timeline and the Detailed Timeline in the back of the book.)

DAY ONE—THESE ARE GOD'S PEOPLE

1. The people rebuilding the walls in Nehemiah are God's people. They have God's word on it. What scriptural

promises to their ancestors apply to these people as a nation?

a.　To Abraham: Genesis 12:1–3 and 13:14–17

b.　To Moses: Exodus 19:3–6

c.　To David: 2 Samuel 7:16

d.　Through the prophet Isaiah: Isaiah 9:6–7

2. The books of Chronicles help here, for they chart the progress of God's people from the beginning to the time of Ezra and Nehemiah. Look at 1 Chronicles 1:1. Why do you think the Chronicler begins where he does?

3. Page through the first eight chapters of 1 Chronicles. What do you notice? In light of the promises of God we have seen, why are these genealogies of God's people so important that, as 1 Chronicles 9:1 says, "All Israel was recorded in genealogies, and these are written in the Book of the Kings of Israel"?

These people we will observe in Nehemiah are God's chosen people from the beginning, Abraham's descendants, destined to become a great nation with an everlasting king on the throne.... What happened? Since Abraham, they had become a nation of many people; they had been delivered out of slavery into the promised land; they had established there a kingdom with some truly great kings. But then all this precious seed of Abraham was scattered, as the kingdom fell apart. What happened?

Day Two—The Consequences of Disobeying God's Law

1. These are God's people, *who show us the consequences of disobeying God's law.* How does 1 Chronicles 9:1b explain? How does Isaiah 1:21–26 amplify?

2. Read the following two summaries, from 2 Kings and 2 Chronicles, of the evils and ends of Israel and Judah. As you read, aim to answer two questions: First, what patterns

of human unfaithfulness do you observe? Second, what do you observe about God's dealing with unfaithfulness?

a. 2 Kings 17:5–15

b. 2 Chronicles 36:11–20

The northern kingdom was dissolved forever, but many Jews from the southern kingdom stayed together, grew, and even prospered in exile—figures such as Daniel and Esther (and Ezra and Nehemiah). A number did remain faithful to their God, and God in his mercy preserved them.

DAY THREE—THE BLESSING OF RECEIVING GOD'S MERCY

These people of God show not only the consequences of disobeying God's law, but also *the blessing of receiving God's mercy*. The very first deportations of Jews from Jerusalem to exile in Babylon had begun as early as 605 B.C. Just short of seventy years later, in 538 B.C., the Jews' free return from exile was decreed by Persian King Cyrus, who had just conquered Judah's conquerors (the Babylonians). This return of God's people to their land is what Ezra and Nehemiah are all about.

1. Read the following verses, first simply to marvel at God's merciful, sovereign hand in this return from exile. Then read them again, and jot down specific observations, surprises, or phrases you want to remember.

    a. Isaiah 44:24–45:13 (This was written by the prophet Isaiah, who lived in the 700s B.C., during the decline and fall of the northern kingdom.)

    b. Jeremiah 25:1–14 (This was written by the prophet Jeremiah, just as the Babylonian invasions of Judah were about to begin.)

c.   2 Chronicles 36:20–23

2. We marvel now, looking back. The prophet Daniel, who had been among the first exiles taken to Babylonia, marveled as he watched it come to pass. What did he do when he read the prophecies from Jeremiah and understood that the end of the exile was near? In Daniel 9:1–19, what can you observe and learn? ("Darius" of v. 1 is probably a temporary ruler appointed over Babylon at the beginning of Cyrus's reign—not the later Persian King Darius.)

Day Four—So What?: Part One

So, we have the background story straight. But what does it have to do with us? Are we simply to benefit from taking in all this fascinating history, or can we begin as well to connect personally with this story? The answer to that last question is a resounding *yes*.

First, *this is our story*, if we have become part of God's people. Most of us probably do not share the privilege of being Jewish, or part of Abraham's physical seed. We could not list our names in the genealogies that continue down through the generations. How can we be part of God's chosen people? What is the only way, ever, for anyone to belong to God?

1. Read Galatians chapter 3. It's a difficult chapter, so we might not understand every part of it—and that is fine. But this chapter answers the question we are asking. The apostle Paul is writing to the Galatians and telling them how to become God's people—and it's not by having Abraham's genes *or* by perfectly obeying the law. So how is it? Write down key phrases from this chapter that point to how we do indeed become God's people, Abraham's true seed.

2. Using some of these key phrases, write your own brief summary of how we become part of God's people, and how it is that this Old Testament story becomes our story.

3. How does the larger biblical story shed light on God's declaration in Isaiah 1:27?

Day Five—So What?: Part Two

Not only is this our story, but, second, *this is our God*. The God of the Bible is one God, from beginning to end, working in all of human history to redeem a people for himself through his Son Jesus Christ. The God to whom we as believers pray when we wake up in the morning is the God to whom Nehemiah prayed when he wanted to go back to Jerusalem. For this final day, look back through the passages we have read during this week of background study. As you reread, jot down key phrases you find that tell you about God—what he is like and how he deals with his people. Spend some time meditating on and worshiping the Lord God.

Notes for Lesson 1

Lesson 2

REBUILDING THE WALLS . . . AGAINST THE BACKGROUND OF EZRA

In Lesson One, we saw the large background story behind Nehemiah. In this lesson, we will see the more immediate background story, from Ezra. Nehemiah actually tells of the *third* group that returns to Jerusalem, while Ezra tells us about the first two groups to return. Just to get it straight:

RETURN #1	RETURN #2	RETURN #3
Led by Zerubbabel to rebuild the temple	Led by Ezra to teach God's people his law	Led by Nehemiah to rebuild the city walls

DAY ONE—RETURN #1: GOD'S PLAN FOR HIS *PEOPLE*

1. Read through Ezra chapter 1. Having done Lesson One, you will notice that we're continuing the story directly

from the Chronicles. What evidences in this chapter do you see of God's sovereign hand in the lives of his people? (Refer to specific verses.)

2. Just *look* at Ezra chapter 2, which carefully counts this first group returning from exile. So much of the seed has been lost because of unfaithfulness, but this faithful number has been preserved and brought back to the land God had given them. Later, in his prayer, how does Ezra repeatedly refer to this group of people, and how does he explain their existence (Ezra 9:6–15)? Write down some further observations about this prayer.

3. Read Isaiah 10:20–23. What similar themes do you find?

4. If we look ahead to the New Testament, we see genealogies are still important. In the genealogy in Matthew's opening chapter, what connections can you find to the postexilic books of Ezra, Nehemiah, and the Chronicles? What would you observe about this line God had promised to preserve?

DAY TWO—RETURN #1:
GOD'S PLAN FOR HIS *TEMPLE*

1. The task of God's people was first to rebuild the temple. Why was this so important? Write down basic

observations concerning the temple, from the following verses:

a. Ezra 3:1–6

b. Ezra 3:10–13

c. 1 Kings 8:1–2, 22–30 (This scene occurs at the dedication of the first temple, built by Solomon.)

2. How would you briefly summarize the role of the temple in the lives of God's people during Old Testament times?

3. When some of Zerubbabel's people wept over the contrast between the simpler new temple and the magnificent old one, God sent his prophet Haggai to encourage them. Read his words in Haggai 2:1–9. What here should encourage the people of God?

4. To what *glory* to come is Haggai ultimately referring (Hag. 2:9)? Before answering, read Luke 2:25–32 and John 1:14.

5. Jesus announced himself as one "greater than the temple" (Matt. 12:6). Read Hebrews 7:23–27, looking to answer this question: Why is Jesus greater than the temple, with all its priests and sacrifices?

DAY THREE—STILL RETURN #1:
GOD'S PLAN FOR *OBSTACLES*

I. In the task of rebuilding the temple, Zerubbabel's group had a great start and then became bogged down . . . for almost twenty years! Summarize the obstacles that arose.

a. Ezra 4:4–5 (an outside problem)

b. Haggai 1:2–9 (an inside problem)

God had a plan for this time and place, obstacles and all. He used kings as one means to carry out his plan. Neighboring officials brought complaints to King Darius against the returned exiles. He looked up King Cyrus's original decree in the Babylonian archives, and ordered the decree (for the Hebrews' return and the temple rebuilding) to be carried out, with the help of all of Judah's neighbors!

2. Read Ezra 6:13–22. In this colorful end to the story of Zerubbabel's group, in what way has God changed the hearts of his people? By what various means is God clearly at work in this passage, accomplishing his good purposes?

3. Read Proverbs 21:1. We've seen how this was true in Ezra. What are the implications of this verse for you, as you try to maneuver what sometimes looks like a course full of obstacles?

DAY FOUR—STILL RETURN #1!:
GOD'S PLAN FOR HIS *WORD*

1. *Prophets* played a crucial role in the postexilic period, as God sent them to keep giving his words to his people. We've read some of God's words through Haggai. Zechariah began his prophetic ministry around the same time (520 B.C.). What are the crucial elements of God's message to Zerubbabel, in Zechariah 4:6–9?

2. In Zechariah 8:1–8, what do the prophet's words tell us of God's *nature* and God's *purposes*?

3. This prophet shows God's purposes reaching all the way through human history. How does Zechariah 9:9–10 reach far, far ahead? (See also Matt. 21:5.)

Day Five—Return #2

1. The last four chapters of Ezra jump ahead probably about sixty years, to the second return of exiles to Jerusalem, led by Ezra. Ezra will be a vital character in the book of Nehemiah, so it is good to get to know him from the start. Write down all you can learn about the man Ezra, from Ezra 7:1–11.

2. According to Ezra 7:12–26, clarify the context of the second return of exiles to Jerusalem. Jot down the *what*, *why*, *how*, and *who* of the assigned mission.

Ezra led his group to Jerusalem. He began to teach the people there God's law, and they began to listen, repent, and obey. Note: The sin that distressed Ezra most was the Hebrews' intermarriage with unbelievers, contrary to God's commands.

3. The scene is now set for us to follow the third return, with Nehemiah. In conclusion to this lesson, as you read the following verses, meditate on God's providential hand over his people through all these journeys. What confidence we can have, that this same God still keeps his hand on his people, for his good purposes! In the following verses, what responses do you see to such a God?

   a. Ezra 7:27–28

b.   Ezra 8:21–23

Notes for Lesson 2

Lesson 3 (*Neh. 1:1–2:10*)

REBUILDING THE WALLS . . .
MEETING THE LEADER

DAY ONE—GETTING INTO THE STORY

The book of Nehemiah tells of the third group of Jewish exiles to return to Jerusalem, in 445 B.C., about 13 years after Ezra led his group. On this first day, do a quick read-through (or even just a careful look-through) of the entire book. Jot down your first impressions concerning this book: tone, possible themes, characters, flow, etc.

(Continued from previous page)

DAY TWO—THE MAIN CHARACTER AND THE MAIN PROBLEM

1. Read Nehemiah 1:1–2:10. Who is telling the story, and what difference does this narrative perspective make to our receiving of it?

The basic fact Nehemiah gives us, in 1:11 (Why does he wait until the end of the chapter?), is that he was *cupbearer* to the Persian King Artaxerxes. A cupbearer was the trusted servant who tasted all the king's food and drink, making sure it was not poisoned. This was no menial position; of the thousands making up the king's household, the cupbearer sat at the king's table, shared his confidence, and even regulated access to the king's presence. That a Jew should rise at this point in history to such a place—*and* that he should be willing to *leave* it—shows the providential working of God.

2. Nehemiah was in Susa, the Persian capital (near the Persian Gulf, in modern-day Iran). He awaited his brother's return from Jerusalem, about 1,000 miles and several months' difficult journey away. Note in Nehemiah 1:2 what *two things* Nehemiah asks his brother, on the brother's return. Then read 1 Chronicles 16:12–18 and Isaiah 62:1–7, and comment on the ways in which

27

these two things represented hope for the Jews. (*Note: Canaan and Zion refer to the promised land, and Mount Zion to Jerusalem as its center.*)

3. The answers to Nehemiah's questions tell of a troubled city. The temple has been rebuilt, but Jerusalem still stands disgraced and defenseless with its broken-down walls. We might ask why broken-down walls and gates would be news, as everyone knew they had been demolished by the Babylonians in 586. Look back to Ezra 4:7–23, which "digresses ahead" and tells an important part of the story behind these walls and the frustrated attempts to rebuild them. Why had Artaxerxes earlier withdrawn his support from this work?

4. Facing this problem is a man we get to know quite personally. From the first sentence of Nehemiah 1:4, what do we learn about Nehemiah?

Day Three—A Man of Prayer

1. Nehemiah did not simply weep. Study the rest of Nehemiah 1:4 carefully, writing down each word or phrase that stands out to you, and briefly noting *why* it stands out.

2. We can read the prayer Nehemiah uttered "day and night" as he waited on God. Read and reread this prayer (Neh. 1:5–11). Then make a simple outline or list of the different parts of the prayer, explaining each one briefly.

For example, I would start with the following as the first of four or five sections:

1) <u>Worship</u> (v. 5): looking up to God and acknowledging who he is: Lord God of heaven, great and awesome, maker and keeper of covenant, source of steadfast love . . .

3. Now, having studied verses 5–11 closely, stand back and make some more general observations about Nehemiah's prayer and the way it might challenge you, as *you* approach the God of heaven.

Spend several minutes in prayer, starting with both praise and confession, and remembering to thank God for the great gift of our Lord Jesus Christ, the Redeemer who came to us through the line of this faithful remnant.

DAY FOUR—A MAN READY TO ACT

1. The prayer recorded in chapter 1 may be the final version of Nehemiah's prayer, as he prays it on the morning of the events of chapter 2, when he knows the time is right to act. The month of Nisan is four months after Chislev (Neh. 1:1), when Nehemiah heard from his brother. As you look over the week's entire passage (1:1–2:10), how

would you say Nehemiah's months of steady prayer prepared him for this day of action?

2. When the time for action arrives, the first thing Nehemiah
   does is to allow himself a sad face. This was a severely
   punishable offense for one in the king's service. Look
   first at the *king's responses* to Nehemiah in this encounter
   (Neh. 2:1–9). How does King Artaxerxes react, and for
   what reasons? (Note specific verses.)

3. Now look at *Nehemiah's* part in this same encounter. What
   characteristics of him are revealed here?

4. Write down your observations of and reactions to each of Nehemiah's addresses to King Artaxerxes:

   a. Nehemiah 2:3

   b. Nehemiah 2:5

   c. Nehemiah 2:7–8

DAY FIVE—CONCLUSIONS

1. What information is inserted in Nehemiah 2:10, and why do you think it is placed at this point in the narrative? (See "People and Places" at the end of this book.)

2. The narrative is set up and ready to go, with the main character, the main problem, and the conflict already in view. In all this, we have begun to grasp Nehemiah's perspective that this story he is telling is most basically the story of *God* graciously working to preserve his people, for his good purposes. To conclude this week's lesson, read and meditate on Isaiah 46:3–13, a passage Nehemiah may have known well, and one that powerfully expresses God's sovereign and redemptive plan for his people. As you read, *write down and meditate on the words of God that stand out to you*, remembering that this is the very God in whom we trust, the one who did send salvation through Jesus Christ, and the one

who continues to accomplish his gracious purposes in the lives of his people.

Notes for Lesson 3

Lesson 4 (Neh. 2:11–3:32)

REBUILDING THE WALLS . . .
How?

DAY ONE—WITH PROPER GROUNDWORK

1. The story moves quickly! The months of travel to Jerusalem go by in a few words, and Nehemiah has arrived in Jerusalem, appointed as governor (see Neh. 5:14). Probably he has all kinds of ideas about how to proceed—but, in Nehemiah 2:11–16, read what he does first. Analyze these verses, and explain the wisdom of each step you see Nehemiah taking.

2. We can only guess what route Nehemiah took for his night outing—although the "Possible Sketch of Nehemiah's Walls" in the back of the book makes a generally accepted suggestion. During Nehemiah's ride, huge piles of rubble probably forced him to dismount. In any case, his private excursion allows him to inspect the site with his own eyes and prepares him to act. But first he needs to prepare the others. As he addresses his fellow Jews, what kinds of appeals does Nehemiah make to cause the people's hearts to burn along with his for the task ahead (Neh. 2:17–18a)?

3. *Derision*, or *dishonor*, or *disgrace* (Neh. 2:17) is something no one desires.

   a. What kinds of disgrace do you see people around you working hardest to avoid?

    b.   Read the following passages, and comment on what kind of disgrace the Bible would teach us to hate?

- Psalm 79:9–10
- Proverbs 30:7–9
- Jeremiah 14:20–21

4. What do you think of the people's response, in Nehemiah 2:18b? How might you explain it?

DAY TWO—WITH CONFIDENCE IN GOD ALONE

1. Enter Sanballat and Tobiah, now joined by Geshem (Neh. 2:19). Review the identities of these men. (See

"People and Places.") What connection did they have to Nehemiah and the people of Judah?

2. The weapons used in Nehemiah 2:19–20 are *words*. Compare and contrast the weapons of the two opposing sides.

3. The source of Nehemiah's confidence is clear throughout Nehemiah 2:20. In what specific ways is this evident?

4. Carefully consider Jesus' words to his disciples in Matthew 5:10–12. What perspective does he give us on suffering insult or persecution for the Lord's sake? What are the truths to hold on to in the midst of such opposition?

5. In light of Nehemiah's example and Christ's own words, what do you or would you ask of God for those today who are suffering insult or persecution because of their faith in Christ? What examples come to mind?

DAY THREE—WITH DILIGENT PLANNING

We've arrived at the kind of chapter we probably skim quickly in the course of our regular Bible reading. As we move through all the unfamiliar names of gates and people and towns, let us look to see the marvelous work of God in every detail of Nehemiah 3.

1. To lead these people in rebuilding, God raised up a man who not only knew how to trust and pray; he also knew how to *plan*—trustingly, prayerfully, and *diligently*. What specific evidences of Nehemiah's thinking and planning have we seen in the first two chapters?

2. His plan apparently divided the wall into 41 sections, which chapter 3 lists counterclockwise, beginning and ending with the Sheep Gate in the northeast corner near the temple (see Neh. 3:1, 32). (The exact location of all the towers and gates is not known, but the "Possible Sketch of Nehemiah's Walls" gives a suggestion.) Consider Nehemiah 3:1. Who are the workers? Why would their presence be significant, if not a little surprising?

How does their described activity set the tone for the whole enterprise?

3. The sections were allotted to the workers not randomly, but with care. What do you notice (and what might be beneficial) about the assignments in Nehemiah 3:10, 23, 28, 29?

4. How do organization and planning go together with faith and trust? How might Nehemiah's story so far challenge you personally in this regard?

DAY FOUR—WITH EVERYBODY INVOLVED

1. Each section of the wall was assigned to a certain group, often with an individual leader. Many of the sections in chapter 3 simply mention individuals' names, but some mention the groups. Look through the chapter, jotting down names of all the groups of workers you find. Then examine and make some observations about the list.

2. Which verse of chapter 3 stands out like a sore thumb, and why?

3. How was Nehemiah different from the Tekoite nobles? What can you discern about him in Nehemiah 2:17, 20 and 4:1, 23?

4. Every person was vitally important, from the governor down to the last daughter or merchant. How does this scene of building apply to us today? We are not building the walls of Jerusalem. The one who was the fulfillment of all the hope of Israel has come. As those who name Jesus Christ as Lord and Savior, *what is our building assignment?* And *what is our role in that assignment?* How do the following verses offer answers to these questions?

   a. Ephesians 4:11–13

b. Romans 12:3–8

DAY FIVE—WHERE ARE YOU IN THIS PICTURE?

1. What a compelling picture of God's people working together for the glory of his name. So often, our hearts and our prayers are set on our own individual tasks, for our own success. Look back through the various passages of this week's study. In what specific ways might these verses affect your prayers?

2. As you think through this week's study one more time, consider the ways in which God uses our obedience, in

any particular moment, for purposes much greater than
we can glimpse. Sum up how this was true for Nehemiah
and his people, and how this is true for us as well. How
does this encourage you and, again, lead you to pray?

Notes for Lesson 4

Lesson 5 (Neh. 4)

REBUILDING THE WALLS . . .
IN SPITE OF OPPOSITION

What should God's people do when they are serving God faithfully, building up his kingdom—and opposition comes? Many Christians around the globe are earnestly asking this question. The providential hand of God allows Sanballats and Tobiahs to attack in a variety of ways. We can learn much from the response of faith in Nehemiah chapter 4.

DAY ONE—ENEMY WEAPON #1: RIDICULE

1. Picture the scene described in Nehemiah 4:1–3. What do you see? What is Sanballat revealing about himself?

2. In Nehemiah 4:2, Sanballat shoots five sharp arrows of verbal attack, which obviously get back to the Jews. What is each arrow (each short question) meant to *do* to the Jews?

3. In what way are the words of Sanballat's sidekick, Tobiah, even more demeaning (Neh. 4:3)?

4. How might you react (or have you perhaps reacted) to such ridicule? List some natural responses.

5. Nehemiah doesn't tell us how he reacted; rather, he acts out his response, reliving the moment for us (Neh. 4:4–5). Ponder this quick instinct to pray. Where in this book have we seen it before? How can we strengthen this instinct in ourselves?

Note: Nehemiah's words in this prayer are difficult, like some of David's in the Psalms when he, too, asks God to punish evil men. The main point in each case is that these men know where to turn for justice, rather than taking it into their own hands. They know that evil really mocks not them but God—so they give it into God's hands.

6. How does the Son of God offer the perfect example to consider, at this point? See 1 Peter 2:19–23.

7. What do you notice, and perhaps even like, about Nehemiah 4:6, which concludes the section?

DAY TWO—ENEMY WEAPON #2: THREAT OF ATTACK

1. The resolution of verse 6 is only temporary. Read Nehemiah 4:7–9. How do the *enemy*, the *weapons*, and the *response* all grow to a higher level?

2. Nehemiah 4:9, concluding this section, is one of the most celebrated verses of Nehemiah.

   a. How does this one sentence show the pattern of Nehemiah's life?

b. In what ways do many people—including you—struggle to keep that pattern in balance? How does this verse challenge you?

3. So far, Nehemiah has referred to God mainly in two ways.

a. What does he call God in Nehemiah 1:4; 1:5; 2:4; and 2:20?

b. What does he call God in Nehemiah 2:8; 2:12; 2:18; 4:4; 4:9; and 4:20?

    c. How is it possible for a person to call the God of heaven "my God" or "our God"? Before answering, read and meditate on Psalm 99.

4. How does Psalm 86:1–7 show what should characterize the prayers of one who knows God as "my God"?

So, again, we picture Nehemiah as he prays, especially in the face of attack. . . . Consider the application of this picture to you.

DAY THREE—ENEMY WEAPON #3: POISONOUS ARROWS OF DISCOURAGEMENT

1. The resolution in verse 9 is temporary as well. Another wave of attack is rising, this time from among the

people, who have been struck by some of the enemy's incoming arrows:

a. Nehemiah 4:10 offers in Hebrew a little saying, a kind of verse the people all begin repeating. What is the source of their discouragement here? In what ways can you identify?

b. Nehemiah 4:11 repeats a threat passed from one person to another. What emotion do you see here, and how do you see its effects?

c. In Nehemiah 4:12, what kind of discouragement is going on? Have you ever met (or perhaps delivered) this kind of discouragement? Briefly explain.

2. Consider: these arrows of discouragement in verses 10–12 are fired not at the beginning, nor the end, but in the middle of the rebuilding project. Why are we often most vulnerable in the *middle*?

3. Comment on the *order* and the *nature* of each part of Nehemiah's response, in Nehemiah 4:13–14.

4. How, practically, does a person banish fear by remembering "the Lord, who is great and awesome"?

5. Why does Nehemiah not tell his people to go out and fight for the *Lord* (Neh. 4:14)?

Day Four—"From That Day On . . ."

1. The chapter's resolution is not that the threat disappears, but that the rebuilding continues in the face of it. With what different words would you describe the people's continuing work, as you observe it specifically in Nehemiah 4:16–23?

2. Repeatedly we are reminded that God is not just watching and listening in this story. How does Nehemiah remind us of this, in Nehemiah 4:15 and 4:20?

3. Examine carefully the pattern of godly leaders, through the following two examples. What similar messages did these leaders give, and how did they call the people to respond?

   a. Exodus 14:10–14

   b. Joshua 23:1–11

4. How would you summarize the connection between our view of God and our daily walk of faith? What implications are here for you?

DAY FIVE—MAY GOD GIVE US SUCH HEARTS

1. In Nehemiah, we are watching a great leader of God's people. His passion, his struggles with opposition, and his unrelenting trust in God might make us think of that great New Testament leader of God's people, Paul. Although one built physical walls of a physical city, and the other helped build the foundations of the church, both fought many of the same battles—ones with which we can identify as well. How do many of the themes of Nehemiah's story repeat themselves in Paul's, in the following passages?

    a. 2 Corinthians 1:8—11

    b. 2 Corinthians 7:2—7

    c. 2 Corinthians 10:1—5

2. These leaders showed hearts burning for the kingdom of God; hearts set on faithful labor for the assigned task; hearts engaged in supernatural warfare against fear and discouragement; hearts full of communion with their Lord God. End this day of study by praying that God would grow such hearts in us and in many leaders of his church today.

Notes for Lesson 5

Lesson 6 (Neh. 5–6)

REBUILDING THE WALLS . . . MORE OPPOSITION

Nehemiah 5 continues the move from a threat outside to a threat inside the walls—and chapter 6 will move back out. Nehemiah offers a powerful picture of faith in God challenged by opposition after opposition, to the very end.

DAY ONE—AN INSIDE PROBLEM

1. Read Nehemiah 5:1–5, and summarize the basic problem (which probably had been simmering long before the wall-building brought it to a crisis).

2. Briefly identify the groups of people involved:

- those complaining (v. 1)

- those complained against (v. 1)

- first group (v. 2)

- second group (v. 3)

- third group (vv. 4–5)

3. According to Leviticus 25:35–43, what parts of the Mosaic law were God's people disobeying?

4. Name each stage of Nehemiah's response to this dis-obedience, addressing each related question as you go.

   a. Nehemiah 5:6 _____
      How would you characterize the proper kind? See Mark 3:5.

   b. Nehemiah 5:7a _____
      Can you give personal testimony to why this stage is crucial?

c. Nehemiah 5:7b–11 _____
   Examine the *way* Nehemiah does this.

d. Nehemiah 5:12b _____
   Why do you think Nehemiah insists on this?

e. Nehemiah 5:13 _____
   What was Nehemiah trying to accomplish here?

Day Two—An "Amen" Response

1. We might do well to identify with the people in this story. Note and comment on their several responses in Nehemiah 5:6–13.

2. "Amen" (v. 13) derives from a Hebrew word connoting surety or faithfulness. Look back to Deuteronomy 27:15–26. Why does God command the people to repeat "Amen" over and over in this passage?

3. Look up and think on the following verses:

   a. Deuteronomy 7:9—literally: "Know therefore that the Lord your God is God; he is the *Amen God*."

   b. Isaiah 55:3—tells, literally, of God's *Amen love* promised to David.

c.   Proverbs 25:13—tells of an *Amen messenger*, trustworthy and pleasing to his master.

d.   John 3:3—offers one of 25 examples in John's gospel where Jesus uses *Amen, amen*, or *Verily, verily*, or *Truly, truly*, to begin an important teaching.

Now, look up and comment on the meaning of 2 Corinthians 1:19–20.

4. Look again at the context of Nehemiah 5:13, as this "Amen" echoes in "all the assembly" of God's people. Why and how is the community of believers so important in teaching us to be "Amen people"?

DAY THREE—THE SIXTH NECESSARY THING

1. We have already seen five "stages" of Nehemiah's response to the people's disobedience. None of these stages would have been effective without the sixth thing he explains to us, in the second part of the chapter. How would you express in a nutshell this sixth thing (Neh. 5:14–19)?

2. How do these same verses reveal Nehemiah's revolutionary perspective on the accustomed rights of a governor appointed by Persian law? What stands out?

3. From these same verses, how can we discern Nehemiah's reasons for living in this way?

4. Look again at Leviticus 25:35–43.

   a. What command is primary here? Sum up the way Nehemiah obeys well this command, in this context.

   b. In what contexts of your life might you struggle to remember the primacy of fearing God, holding him and no one else as your audience and your judge?

DAY FOUR—REENTER VILLAINS

The wall keeps rising, until it's all done but the gate doors. The surrounding enemies are afraid and try two more evil tactics, against Nehemiah personally. For each one, after reading the background notes, carefully study Nehemiah's response and write down specific evidences of wise and godly behavior.

1. Nehemiah 6:1–9
   Notes:
   - The Plain of Ono (*v. 2*) was about a day's journey northwest, right on the edge of Sanballat's territory. A pretty obvious trap.
   - The "unsealed letter" (*v. 5*) was probably either an inscribed oblong of clay pottery, or else an unsealed papyrus. The point is that the slanderous contents were read by everybody around.

2. Nehemiah 6:10–14
   Notes:
   - Shemaiah was a corrupt prophet manipulated by Sanballat and Tobiah.
   - The last words of *v. 10*, in the Hebrew, constitute a poetic oracle which Shemaiah probably chanted ominously.
   - The sin into which Shemaiah meant to entice Nehemiah was that of entering the temple unlawfully. Only Levitical priests were allowed inside the temple (Num. 18:7). Years before, King Uzziah had entered, and was struck with leprosy (2 Chron. 26:19).

Day Five—Done!

1. After all this, how does Nehemiah 6:15 strike you?

2. According to Nehemiah 6:16, what was one significant part of God's purpose in drawing a ring of enemy nations around Judah? How might this affect your perspective on the world today?

3. Is all the opposition finally stilled? What do you observe in Nehemiah 6:17–19?

4. God led his people to rebuild the walls of Jerusalem in the face of tremendous opposition. Look briefly through last week's lesson and this one, and recall several high points, *spiritually*, for God's people, in the midst of struggle and strife.

5. What might this part of the story encourage you to do and to pray, as you and as God's people face various kinds of opposition?

Finish by meditating on Nehemiah's words: "Don't be afraid of them. Remember the Lord, who is great and awesome" (Neh. 4:14).

73

Notes for Lesson 6

Lesson 7 (Neh. 7–8)

The Walls Rebuilt . . .
Around God's People
and God's Word

Day One—The People Are the Thing

1. Even with the walls rebuilt, Nehemiah's work is not finished. In Nehemiah 7:1–5, how does this leader exhibit the same wise and godly qualities in the reorganization as he did in the rebuilding?

With the temple and the city safely in operating order, Nehemiah turns his attention to the people for whom these structures have been raised. He tells of assembling and registering them by families. He gives us the genealogical record he found from the first group that returned, under Zerubbabel (see Neh. 7:5–73). Evidently he used this older document to organize and enroll everyone who had since arrived. Nehemiah 7 is a close repeat of Ezra 2.

2. Why do you think Nehemiah chose at this point to reinforce the family roots of those dwelling in the land?

3. Look through chapter 7 and think back to where we started and where we've come. Look ahead through chapter 8. In what ways is this a turning point in the book, and in what ways have we been prepared for what comes next? (See "Outline of Nehemiah" at the end of the book.)

With chapter 8, Nehemiah disappears as narrator, not to take up the story himself again until Nehemiah 12:27. Nehemiah, a layman, has done his job of preparing the way for the priest Ezra. Ezra has been in Judah since 458, teaching and instructing the people, but not until this climactic point are the people enabled and prepared to stand together publicly, ready to hear God's Word to them.

DAY TWO—GATHERING THE PEOPLE AND GETTING THE PICTURE

1. We must imagine the grand scene. What observations would you make about *who* gathered and *where* they gathered (Neh. 8:1–3)?

This gate was on Jerusalem's eastern side, overlooking the Kedron Valley, where the city's principal source of water (the Gihon Spring) was located. Across the valley rose the Mount of Olives.

2. *When* (on the calendar) and *when* (in the day) did they gather (Neh. 8:2–3)? What practical preparations must have been made?

Read Leviticus 23:23–25. Jews now celebrate this day as the Jewish New Year—Rosh Hashanah.

3. What would you observe about the focal point of this gathering (Neh. 8:1–3)?

Picture the high platform (literally "tower") on which stands Ezra, with six men to his right and seven men to his left (to help him read). Thousands of faces—children, parents, and grandparents—turn upward, lighted by the rising sun, straining to catch every word.

4. What do you observe about the people's attitude toward the Book of the Law of Moses, in Nehemiah 8:1–5? Compare and contrast their attitudes with those you see in and around you today.

DAY THREE—THE PEOPLE RESPOND
TO THE BOOK

1. What important elements of worship do you observe in Nehemiah 8:6?

2. Thirteen Levites (See "People and Places in Nehemiah") walked among the people.

   a. Write the phrases that describe what these Levites did and what they were after (Neh. 8:7–8).

   b. What implications might we draw here concerning the Word of God?

c. In what ways (especially those ways suggested by the story!) can each of us make progress in understanding and getting the sense of biblical texts?

3. A triple question: In Nehemiah 8:9–11, what do you observe about the people's response to God's Word? What do you observe about the leaders' response to their response? How do *you* respond to these responses?

4. "The joy of the Lord is your *strength*" (Neh. 8:10). That word is often translated "stronghold" or "fortress."

   a. Having just worked so hard on physical walls, what is Nehemiah pointing out here?

   b. What *is* the joy of the Lord? To help in your answer, read Nehemiah 8:12 and Isaiah chapter 12.

   c. How does Nehemiah direct the people to *express* their joy, in this passage?

DAY FOUR—THE PEOPLE PAY ATTENTION
TO THE BOOK

1. How did the next day's events show that the people had truly committed themselves to this book (Neh. 8:13)?

2. Using Nehemiah 8:13–18, carefully observe and explain how this group models the ways in which God's people should interact with God's Word. Write down your thoughts, including any practical implications or applications that occur to you.

   Note: The Feast of Booths was established by God for the Israelites to celebrate annually, both as a harvest feast and as a memorial of their wandering in the wilderness with no permanent home, after God had delivered them from Egypt. This second aspect, involving the building of temporary shelters, had been forgotten for years.

Day Five—You and the Book

1. On this day, spend some time thinking and praying about the place God's Word holds in your life. You might consider these questions:

   - What is my attitude toward the Word of God?
   - Do I pay attention to it daily?
   - Do I study it in order to understand it clearly?
   - Do I submit myself to the teaching of my God-ordained leaders?
   - Do I listen to it and discuss it regularly in the assembly of God's people?
   - Does reading God's Word affect my heart—in conviction, in praise, in joy?
   - Do I work to obey what the Bible tells me to do?

83

2. Pray, with the psalmist, the words from Psalm 119:33–37—
   or the entire psalm, if you have time! Write down any
   phrases you want to remember or consider further.

Notes for Lesson 7

Lesson 8 (Neh. 9–10)

THE WALLS REBUILT . . .
A TIME TO CONFESS
AND COMMIT

The joyful Feast of Tabernacles ended on the twenty-second day of the month. God's people had together heard, celebrated, and obeyed the Word of God. Joy had properly replaced weeping at that momentous celebration. The impulse to weep, however, had been a good one. Two days later, before scattering to their homes, the people completed their time together with one final worship session of confession and commitment.

DAY ONE—CONFESSION BEFORE THE LORD

1. The people had obviously intended and prepared to spend time in confession before God, as we see in Nehemiah 9:1. What should we learn and not learn from their example?

2. In Psalm 51:16–17, what does David say are the most important things to bring to God in confession?

3. Notice the very next prayer of David, in Psalm 51:18–19. In light of our Nehemiah study, what do you note in David's prayers for Jerusalem? What is he asking here?

4. Nehemiah 9:2a describes not simply racial but religious separation. It is crucial to note that foreigners who put their faith in God, such as Rahab and Ruth, became part of God's people (see Ezra 6:21). But this is not primarily

what had been happening in Judah, as Ezra found out when he arrived (see Ezra 9:1–4).

a.   Why had God told his people not to marry foreign-ers, according to Exodus 34:15–16?

b.   Why do you think we are told of their obedience in this respect at this point in the narrative (Neh. 9:2)?

5.   Confession involves more than simply telling God all about oneself. Observe and comment on the way the Israelites organized this half-day event (Neh. 9:3). (A quarter of the day would be 3 hours.)

Day Two—Making It Clear

1. The people are probably led again by Ezra and by two choirs of Levites, on the stairs on either side of the wooden platform (Neh. 9:4–5). Their ringing call (v. 5) is a summons to focus on the Lord God, and that is just what this, the longest prayer in the Bible, does. To get started, read through the first large section (Neh. 9:5–31). What central theme or idea do you find developed?

2. To understand this prayer more clearly, we will go back and read carefully, in sections. As you examine each of the following five sections, write down a summary of:

   • What part of biblical history is covered
   • What you learn of God
   • What you learn of God's people

   a. Nehemiah 9:5–6

b.   Nehemiah 9:7–8

c.   Nehemiah 9:9–11

d.   Nehemiah 9:12–21

e.   Nehemiah 9:22–31

DAY THREE—NOW THEREFORE . . .

1. Nehemiah 9:32–37 is the sixth and last section of the prayer, as verse 32 brings the prayer to Nehemiah's own time.

    a.   How does this section beautifully summarize all that has gone before?

    b.   How do the people show in this section that they are confessing their own sins, not just the sins of others?

c. Why is it often so difficult to acknowledge and confess clearly our own sins? Why must we?

2. What are the people mainly asking of God in this prayer
of chapter 9?

3. In this same month, the Jews would have also celebrated
the annual Day of Atonement, when the high priest
offered sacrifices for all the sins of the Israelites. These
people knew that their sin had to be forgiven in order
for them to be acceptable to a holy God. They knew
that "without the shedding of blood there is no forgive-
ness" (Heb. 9:22). They didn't know the name of the
one toward whom all their sacrifices were pointing. But
in faith they humbly and obediently confessed before
their merciful God. What a wonder, to think that we
can confess like them and name the name of Jesus,
who offered himself as the final, perfect sacrifice for

our sins. Read Hebrews 9:23–28. How does this passage clarify what Jesus came to do in regard to our sin? How should such certainties, received by faith, affect our process of confession?

DAY FOUR—FROM CONFESSION TO COMMITMENT

1. Read through Nehemiah 10, where the scene of prayer continues. Earnest confession leads to *what*, in chapter 10? How does this progression make sense? How have you perhaps experienced or observed this connection?

2. What importance do you see in the steps taken to make the people's commitment binding (Neh. 9:38–10:27)?

3. Not just the leadership, but all the people solemnly bind themselves to this commitment—which is generally to obey the Word of God (Neh. 10:28–29). Summarize the specific parts of the Word they emphasize:

    a. Nehemiah 10:30

    b. Nehemiah 10:31

    c. Nehemiah 10:32–39

4. Would God's people be able to keep this oath of commitment? We shall see, in a few chapters. As the years passed, they did maintain a focus on the law of God—although they became prideful in their efforts to obey. What did they—and what do we—need to be reminded to do, as we see in Matthew 3:1–6?

Day Five—Doing It

Such *time* God's people took in the presence of the Lord in these chapters! Let us take some time ourselves on this last day to confess before God who he is and who we are—sinners in need of his grace, which was fully shown in the sacrifice of Jesus Christ for us on the cross. Take some minutes to look back through these chapters, to look up to the Lord God, to confess, and to commit ourselves in faith to the one God promised would come through Abraham's seed. According to God's Word, he came, he died, he rose, and he will come again to judge the world. Praise God that he is perfectly faithful to his promises! Praise God that he listens to us as we come to him with specific words of prayer!

Notes for Lesson 8

Lesson 9 (Neh. 11:1–13:3)

THE WALLS REBUILT . . .
AND DEDICATED

DAY ONE—SETTLING IN

1. Chapter 11 concerns itself with recording the various people who inhabited Jerusalem and the towns in Judah. Again, we must be struck with the careful counting of this remnant of the seed of Abraham, the people of the promise in the place God had promised them. The first concern in this chapter is with *Jerusalem*. What is the issue needing attention, and why would it be important (Neh. 11:1–2)?

The remnant probably included representatives from most or even all of the original twelve tribes of Israel (descended from the sons of Jacob). But the great majority of the group comes from three tribes—Judah, Benjamin, and Levi—all of whom were original inhabitants of the southern kingdom of Judah. The tribes of Judah and Benjamin had been assigned territory there; many priests and Levites lived there to be close to the temple, where they worked. (Priests and Levites were both in Levi's tribe; only descendants of Aaron were priests.)

2. Look again to Matthew 1:1–3 for a reminder of which tribe would produce Jesus Christ. How do the following verses give a glimpse of God's great plan for this tribe?

a. Genesis 49:8–10 (The scene: old Jacob's blessing of his sons before he dies)

b. Micah 5:2

c. Revelation 5:5

3. God had a plan for each of the tribes. For example, think about the descendants of Levi, so prominent in these chapters of Nehemiah. Ever since Moses' day, they had been given the priestly or priestly related work. They had never been given territory of their own. How does Deuteronomy 18:1–5 explain this?

4. After the exile, this landless tribe is prospering and continuing to minister in the name of the Lord their inheritance. From the two following passages, list some of the Levites' many diverse tasks relating to the temple, the center of life in Jerusalem.

   a.   Nehemiah 11:15–23

   b.   1 Chronicles 9:22–33

5. Finally, on this day, just look through Nehemiah 11:25–
   12:26. You are looking at lists of: (1) towns inhabited by
   the descendants of various tribes, and (2) generations
   of priests and Levites. At the least we can marvel at the
   orderly recording of so many seemingly insignificant
   people and places, each of which had a crucial spot in
   the unfolding of God's plan.

Day Two—Get Ready for the Music!

1. The people of God come together once again, this time
   to dedicate the restored walls of Jerusalem! What preparations must have taken place in the preceding weeks,
   just from what you can tell in Nehemiah 12:27–29?

2. It's not surprising that music is mentioned first in connection with celebration, is it? Briefly, what part does
   music play in the following celebrations?

   a.   Job 38:4–7

b.   Exodus 15:1, 20—21

c.   2 Chronicles 5:2—3, 12—14

d.   Revelation 5:11—13

3. Nehemiah 12:31 speaks of two great "choirs that gave
    thanks." That phrase (also in v. 38 and v. 40) translates
    one Hebrew word meaning "thanksgiving." What do these
    choirs make you think and picture?

4. Although music is beautiful to a person in solitude, how is music especially important and fitting for the whole gathering of God's people?

DAY THREE—PURIFICATION BEFORE CELEBRATION

1. Other preparations take place as well, including ceremonial purification (Neh. 12:30).

   a. What sorts of preparatory purification activities, for example, do we find in Exodus 19:10–15?

   b. Why is it crucial for us to confess and have a clean heart before entering into worship with God's people in God's presence?

2. Can you remember (and describe briefly) an occasion when you tried to worship with God's people *and* harbor sin at the same time?

3. How does Psalm 24:3–4 describe one who may come into the presence of the Lord?

4. Right on the heels of that last question, however, we must affirm again the way in which we are made clean. What is the promise of I John 1:9?

DAY FOUR—BIG-TIME CELEBRATION

1. Nehemiah is back in first-person narration (Neh. 12:31), directing the show! Read Nehemiah 12:31–42 and make yourself some kind of simple outline or drawing to put together all these stage directions. (The two groups probably started at the Valley Gate, as Nehemiah had done on that early night ride.)

2. Nehemiah 12:43 overflows with *joy*. Write down everything you can notice about *joy* in this verse.

3. Imagine the sound, as the last sentence of verse 43 describes it. What is it like?

4. In what ways should the *joy* of God's people be an audible and noticeable witness to the world around us? (Recall also Neh. 8:10–12.)

5. Read and meditate on Psalm 126. This psalm of joy was perhaps specifically for the returned exiles, but it certainly is for all God's people. Write down particular phrases you want to think about and remember.

DAY FIVE—THE WAY IT'S SUPPOSED TO WORK

1. Looking at Nehemiah 12:44–47, how would you describe the city and Nehemiah's attitude toward it, as he gives this summary view?

2. Read Nehemiah 13:1–3. Read also Deuteronomy 23:3–6 (as they evidently were doing) for background. This passage offers another example of the crucial issue explained in Lesson 8, Day 1. Why do you think this section is carefully inserted at this point? (*Note: Balaam was a pagan prophet whom God chose to use so that blessings on Israel came out of his mouth, rather than the curses for which he had been hired—story in Numbers 22–24.*)

3. This book has consistently shown us God's people in community—working together, repenting together, worshiping together, rejoicing together. *That God's people together might obey and honor God* has been Nehemiah's passion throughout. Think back through the whole story

and write a list of application questions for yourself,
dealing specifically with the ways in which you live as
a member of God's people—now the body of Christ.
Then examine and prayerfully consider what you have
written. For example, your list might include questions
like this:

- Do I pray earnestly and regularly for God's people?
- How far would I travel and how long would I stand
  to take in the Word of God?
- Is worship with God's people a priority and a joy
  for me?

Notes for Lesson 9

Lesson 10 (Neh. 13:4–31)

THE WALLS REBUILT . . . WHEN WILL THE LIGHT SHINE?

The previous chapter (Nehemiah 12) would have made a great conclusion for Nehemiah. Such joyful resolution . . . which throughout the Old Testament, however, always seems to come with a "but." Nehemiah 13, the last chapter, gives a large "but," bringing Nehemiah back for one more fiery appearance to deal with the people of God. After twelve years as governor of Judah, Nehemiah had returned to Susa. It's not clear how long he was gone. But when he returns, three large confrontations occur, concerning issues with which Nehemiah has already dealt. The ending of Nehemiah is not all light and joy. When will the light finally shine for the people of God?

DAY ONE—ABOUT THE HOUSE OF GOD

1. It's Tobiah again. (We knew, at the end of chapter 6, that he'd resurface.) Read Nehemiah 13:4–14.

a. Who was responsible for what evil thing here, and what further wrongs resulted?

b. Outline and comment on Nehemiah's very thorough course of action in response. (Don't you feel you really know this man by this point?)

2. How did the prophet Malachi, in Nehemiah's time, speak directly to this situation? See Malachi 2:7–9; 3:6–12.

3. Read John 2:13–17. What is the motivation behind both Nehemiah's and Jesus' zeal?

4. Look back to Nehemiah 10:37–39. What strikes you?

DAY TWO—ABOUT THE SABBATH

1. Read Nehemiah 13:15–22, and then look back to Nehemiah 10:31. What strikes you?

2. Look farther back, as Nehemiah is doing in Nehemiah 13:18. Read Jeremiah 17:19–27. What do you observe in these words of the prophet Jeremiah to the people of Judah, long before?

3. Look farther back, to Exodus 20:8–11 and 31:12–17. How does the importance of this issue stand out?

4. How do we recognize Nehemiah again in the various aspects of his response (Neh. 13:15–22)?

DAY THREE—ABOUT MARRIAGES WITH UNGODLY FOREIGNERS

1. We have met this issue again and again, as God's people repeatedly disobey the command to keep themselves holy, set apart for the holy Lord God. (Again, see Lesson 8, Day 1, for further clarification.) Read Nehemiah 13:23–31, and then look back to Nehemiah 10:30. What strikes you?

2. Nehemiah refers to Solomon's example (Neh. 13:26). Read the clear facts, in 1 Kings 11:1–8. Why is Solomon's example such a powerful one?

3. Now, turn again to Malachi. How does this prophet of Nehemiah's day regard the issue of marriages with unbelieving foreigners (Mal. 2:10–12)?

4. In Nehemiah 13:24, why do you think Nehemiah mentions the language of the Jewish children?

5. Yes, Nehemiah gets a bit heated in his response (Neh. 13:25).

   a. Contrast *his* response to *Ezra's* (Ezra 9:1–15).

   b. In what ways do we as the people of God today allow a passionless tolerance of sin to creep into our lives?

6. Consider the book's final two verses.

    a. What would you say is the motivation driving Nehemiah to the end?

    b. With what kind of resolution does the book end? How does the end of the book feel to you?

Day Four—Prayers that Look Up and Ahead

1. Nehemiah has faithfully shown what it means to live and operate in the very presence of God, as his final prayer and his regularly inserted prayers of all kinds attest. To review the consistent thread of prayer, look back to Nehemiah's interspersed prayers in chapters 4–6, as well as the four prayers throughout chapter 13. What do you see as Nehemiah's consistent desire in his prayers?

(To help with the meaning of God's "remembering," see Genesis 8:1 and 1 Samuel 1:19.)

2. Looking back over the book, how would you summarize the connection between Nehemiah's prayers and Nehemiah's actions.

Nehemiah's final prayers reach out with longing for the Lord God. The sense that God is yet to act, and the longing for him to do so, permeates the Old Testament, becoming even stronger in the later prophets. To his people God had promised glory, salvation, an everlasting king in the line of David, justice, blessing for all nations. . . . When would the promise be fulfilled? When would the light finally shine? Each time the light of the promise seemed close—in the Exodus, in the united kingdom, in the return from exile—*each time*, sin came in and darkened the picture.

The promise remained, though, and God was accomplishing it. The light never went out, even when the people couldn't see it. God raised up prophets and leaders to point to the light and call the people to follow it. There were always a few who did; there was always a faithful remnant to carry on the seed and trace God's covenant promises.

3. When the full light dawned, did God's people recognize and welcome it, after all this waiting? How would you answer, according to the following passages?

   a. Luke 2:25–32

   b. John 1:1–11

   c. John 3:16–21

4. Let us remind ourselves: Who are God's true people, according to the passages just read?

5. And where are God's true people to dwell, according to God's promises? As you read the following passages, simply write down phrases that describe the Jerusalem that is promised, throughout Scripture, to God's people. We will not try to explain everything in these verses; we will try to get a picture, gain a glimpse of the dwelling that is our hope, as the people of God. Many passages like these deal with the historical city of Jerusalem, as we have seen, while at the same time reaching forward and dealing with a future city as well.

   a. Isaiah 60:10–22

   b. Zechariah 14:6–11

   c. Hebrews 12:22–24

   d. Revelation 21:1–4, 22–27

DAY FIVE—LIVING IN THE LIGHT

When the light broke fully, in Jesus Christ, he illumined all of history, past and future. We can look back and see that light shining on Nehemiah, showing us his faithful part in preparing the way for the Redeemer to come to the place and through the lineage God had promised. In his obedience and faith, Nehemiah was building to welcome a King and establish a city, both far greater than he ever dreamed.

1. For us who have believed in Christ, the light shines behind us and before us. All of God's promises are fulfilled in Christ, but not all of them have come to pass in human history. What will happen before God's people inhabit that heavenly city? From the following verses, write down phrases that tell us about some of the promises concerning Christ Jesus still to be fulfilled.

   a. Hebrews 9:27–28

   b. John 14:1–3

    c.   Acts 1:6–11

2. In the meantime, as we look forward to that day, we are to be building faithfully and obediently as well. Even though our city is invisible right now, we have incredible resources to do the building—the army and the resources of the King of kings. Relish the following two passages, in light of all we have studied: 1 Peter 2:4–10 and Ephesians 2:19–22. Then, in conclusion, write down for yourself a summary of your building project as a member of the body of Christ.

3. Finally, have you memorized the Scripture passages for this study? (See p. 141.) Say these verses aloud or read them aloud, prayerfully, on this last day. May we go away from our study of Nehemiah with joy, having understood God's Word to us.

Notes for Lesson 10

NOTES FOR LEADERS

What a privilege it is to lead a group in studying the Word of God! Following are six principles offered to help guide you as you lead.

1. THE PRIMACY OF THE BIBLICAL TEXT

If you forget all the other principles, I encourage you to hold on to this one! The Bible is God speaking to us, through his inspired Word—living and active and sharper than a two-edged sword. As leaders, we aim to point people as effectively as possible into this Word. We can trust the Bible to do all that God intends in the lives of those studying with us.

This means that the job of a leader is to direct the conversation of a group constantly back into the text. If you "get stuck," usually the best thing to say is: "Let's go back to the text and read it again. . . ." The questions in this study aim to lead people into the text, rather than into a swirl of personal opinions about the topics of the text; therefore, depending on the questions should help. Personal opinions and experiences will often enrich your group's interactions; however, many Bible studies these days have moved almost exclusively into the realm of "What does this mean to me?" rather than first trying to get straight on "What does this mean?"

We'll never understand the text perfectly, but we can stand on one of the great principles of the Reformation: the *perspicuity* of Scripture. This simply means *understandability*. God made us word-creatures, in his image, and he gave us a Word that he wants us to understand more and more, with careful reading and study, and shared counsel and prayer.

The primacy of the text implies less of a dependence on commentaries and answer guides than often has been the case. I do not offer answers to the questions, because the answers are in the biblical text, and we desperately need to learn how to dig in and find them. When individuals articulate what they find for themselves (leaders included!), they have learned more, with each of their answers, about studying God's Word. These competencies are then transferable and applicable in every other study of the Bible. Without a set of answers, a leader will not be an "answer person," but rather a fellow searcher of the Scriptures.

Helps *are* helpful in the right place! It is good to keep at hand a Bible dictionary of some kind. The lessons themselves actually offer context and help with the questions as they are asked. A few commentaries are listed in the "Notes on Translations and Study Helps," and these can give further guidance after one has spent good time with the text itself. I place great importance as well on the help of leaders and teachers in one's church, which leads us into the second principle.

2. THE CONTEXT OF THE CHURCH

As Christians, we have a new identity: we are part of the body of Christ. According to the New Testament, that body is clearly meant to live and work in local bodies, local churches. The ideal context for Bible study is within a church body—one that is reaching out in all directions to the people around it. (Bible studies can be the best places for evangelism!) I realize that these

studies will be used in all kinds of ways and places; but whatever
the context, I would hope that the group leaders have a layer of
solid church leaders around them, people to whom they can go
with questions and concerns as they study the Scriptures. When
a leader doesn't know the answer to a question that arises, it's
really OK to say, "I don't know. But I'll be happy to try to find
out." Then that leader can go to pastors and teachers, as well as
to commentaries, to learn more.

The church context has many ramifications for Bible study.
For example, when a visitor attends a study and comes to know
the Lord, the visitor—and his or her family—can be plugged into
the context of the church. For another example, what happens
in a Bible study often can be integrated with other courses of
study within the church, and even with the preaching, so that
the whole body learns and grows together. This depends, of
course, on the connection of those leading the study with those
leading the church—a connection that I have found to be most
fruitful and encouraging.

3. THE IMPORTANCE OF PLANNING
AND THINKING AHEAD

How many of us have experienced the rush to get to Bible
study on time . . . or have jumped in without thinking through
what will happen during the precious minutes of group interac-
tion . . . or have felt out of control as we've made our way through
a quarter of the questions and used up three-quarters of the time!

It is crucial, after having worked through the lesson yourself,
to think it through from the perspective of leading the discussion. How will you open the session, giving perhaps a nutshell
statement of the main theme and the central goals for the day?
(Each lesson offers a brief introduction that will help with the
opening.) Which questions do you not want to miss discussing,
and which ones could you quickly summarize or even skip? How

much time would you like to allot for the different sections of the study?

If you're leading a group by yourself, you will need to prepare extra carefully—and that can be done! If you're part of a larger study, perhaps with multiple small groups, it's helpful for the various group leaders to meet together and to help each other with the planning. Often, a group of leaders meets early on the morning of a study, in order to help the others with the fruit of their study, plan the group time, and pray—which leads into the fourth principle.

4. The Crucial Role of Prayer

If these words we're studying are truly the inspired Word of God, then how much we need to ask for his Spirit's help and guidance as we study his revelation! This is a prayer found often in Scripture itself, and a prayer God evidently loves to answer: that he would give us understanding of his truth, according to his Word. I encourage you as a leader to pray before and as you work through the lesson, to encourage those in your group to do the same, to model this kind of prayer as you lead the group time, to pray for your group members by name throughout the week, and to ask one or two "prayer warriors" in your life to pray for you as you lead.

5. The Sensitive Art of Leading

Whole manuals, of course, have been written on this subject! Actually, the four principles preceding this one may be most fundamental in cultivating your group leadership ability. Again, I encourage you to consider yourself not as a person with all the right answers, but rather as one who studies along with the people in your group—and who then facilitates the group members' discussion of all they have discovered in the Scriptures.

There is always a tension between pouring out the wisdom of all your own preparation and knowledge, on the one hand, and encouraging those in your group to relish and share all they have learned, on the other. I advise leaders to lean more heavily toward the latter, reserving the former to steer gently and wisely through a well-planned group discussion. What we're trying to accomplish is not to cement our own roles as leaders, but to participate in God's work of raising up mature Christians who know how to study and understand the Word—and who will themselves become equipped to lead.

With specific issues in group leading—such as encouraging everybody to talk, or handling one who talks too much—I encourage you to seek the counsel of one with experience in leading groups. There is no better help than the mentoring and prayerful support of a wise person who has been there! That's even better than the best "how-to" manual. If you have a number of group leaders, perhaps you will invite an experienced group leader to come and conduct a practical session on how to lead.

Remember: the default move is, "Back to the text!"

6. THE POWER OF THE SCRIPTURES TO DELIGHT

Finally, in the midst of it all, let us not forget to delight together in the Scriptures! We should be serious but not joyless! In fact, we as leaders should model for our groups a growing and satisfying delight in the Word of God—as we notice its beauty, stop to linger over a lovely word or phrase, enjoy the poetry, appreciate the shape of a passage from beginning to end, laugh at a touch of irony or an image that hits home, wonder over a truth that pierces the soul.

May we share and spread the response of Jeremiah, who said:

> Your words were found, and I ate them,
>   and your words became to me a joy
>   and the delight of my heart. (Jer. 15:16)

Outline of Nehemiah

I. The Plot Is Established

Nehemiah returns to Jerusalem to rebuild the walls (Neh. 1–2)

II. The Plot Develops

In spite of opposition, the walls are rebuilt (Neh. 3–6)

    Interval: Documenting the Organization of City and People (Neh. 7)

III. The Plot Resolves

God's people hear and obey God's Word (Neh. 8:1–13:3)

  A. Covenant Renewal around the Word of God (Neh. 8–10)

    Interval: Documenting the Organization of City and People (Neh. 11:1–12:26)

  B. Dedication of the Wall (Neh. 12:27–43)

  C. God's People Obeying the Law (Neh. 12:44–13:3)

IV. The Plot "Un-Resolves"

Nehemiah confronts continued sin among God's people (Neh. 13:4–31)

Timelines and Geography of Nehemiah's World

- General Timeline
- Detailed Timeline
- Map of Nehemiah's World
- Possible Sketch of Nehemiah's Walls

General Timeline

Timelines reflect best approximations of commentators referenced in the Notes.

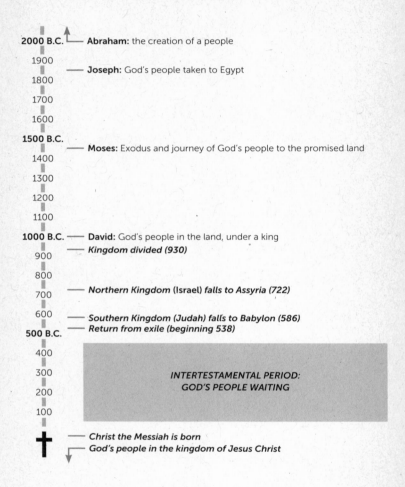

2000 B.C. — **Abraham:** the creation of a people

1900

1800 — **Joseph:** God's people taken to Egypt

1700

1600

1500 B.C.

1400 — **Moses:** Exodus and journey of God's people to the promised land

1300

1200

1100

1000 B.C. — **David:** God's people in the land, under a king

900 — *Kingdom divided (930)*

800

700 — *Northern Kingdom (Israel) falls to Assyria (722)*

600 — *Southern Kingdom (Judah) falls to Babylon (586)*

500 B.C. — *Return from exile (beginning 538)*

400

300 *INTERTESTAMENTAL PERIOD: GOD'S PEOPLE WAITING*

200

100

✝ — *Christ the Messiah is born*
— *God's people in the kingdom of Jesus Christ*

Detailed Timeline
for Ezra and Nehemiah

Approximations, generally accepted

	Events	King
600 B.C.		
	586: *Judah captured and taken into exile by Babylonians. Jerusalem and its temple destroyed.*	**Nebuchadnezzar**—*Babylonian*
550		
	539: *King Cyrus takes over Babylon and decrees that Jewish exiles may return to their land. Zerubbabel in 538 leads the first return and begins to rebuild the temple.*	**Cyrus**—*Persian*
	536-520: *Temple rebuilding halts.*	**Cambyses**—*Persian*
	516: *With encouragement of prophets Haggai and Zechariah, the temple is finally completed.*	**Darius**—*Persian*
500 B.C.		
	486–464: *Esther's reign as queen takes place during this period.*	**Xerxes I**—*Persian*
450	*458:* *Ezra leads the second return and teaches God's people the Law.*	**Artaxerxes**—*Persian*
	445: *Nehemiah leads the third return and rebuilds Jerusalem's walls. He and Ezra lead the people in worship and rededication to the Lord.*	
400 B.C.		

135

Map of Nehemiah's World

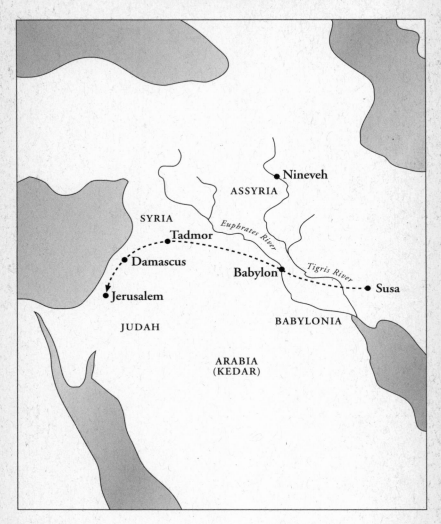

From Susa (the Persian Capital) to Jerusalem was about 1,000 miles—a journey of several months.

Possible Sketch of Nehemiah's Walls

Reflects best approximations of commentators referenced in the Notes.

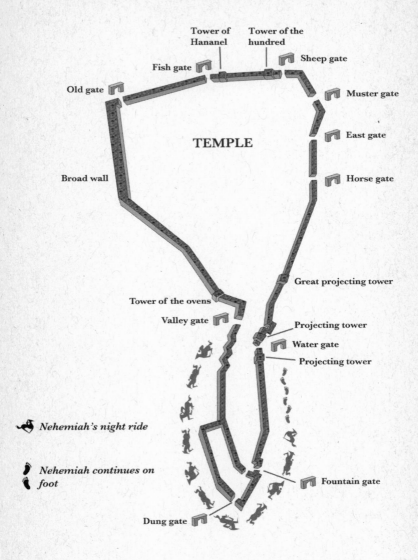

PEOPLE AND PLACES
IN NEHEMIAH

Artaxerxes	King of Persia 464–424 B.C.—helped both Ezra and Nehemiah. Nicknamed "Longimanus" or "Long-handed," his right hand being longer than his left.
Babylonia	Territory in southwest Asia, now Iraq, called after its capital city Babylon. The Babylonians, who grew into a great empire, conquered Judah in 586 B.C. (led by King Nebuchadnezzar) and took its people into exile.
Ezra	A Jewish priest, learned scribe, and teacher of the law who led the second return of exiles to Jerusalem. He turned God's people back to God's Word.
Geshem	Leader of powerful group of Arab communities to the south and east of Judah. Opposed Nehemiah.
Israel	1. The new name God gave to Jacob, or 2. The whole nation of people who trace their ancestry to Jacob's 12 sons, or 3. The northern kingdom, with Samaria as its capital, which was conquered by the Assyrians in 722 B.C. Its people were exiled and dispersed.
Jerusalem	Capital city of Judah, called "the holy city," with the temple at its center.

Judah	1. The fourth son of Jacob, after whom was named one of the tribes of Israel, or 2. The name of the southern kingdom, the area restored after the exile.
Levites	Descendants of Levi (Jacob's son) who served the temple in all non-priestly capacities. They were supported by tithes from God's people. The *priests* were members of Levi's tribe as well, but had to be descendants of Moses' brother Aaron, the first high priest.
Nehemiah	A Jew who rose to political leadership in the Persian Empire, as cupbearer to King Artaxerxes and then as governor of Judah. He led the third group of exiles returning to Jerusalem, to rebuild its walls.
Persia	Territory east of the Persian Gulf with Susa as its capital. It grew into a great empire after the Babylonians fell. Persian King Cyrus conquered the Babylonians and decreed in 538 B.C. the free return of Jews to their land.
Sanballat	Leader of Nehemiah's opponents. He was governor of Samaria, to the north of Judah.
Tobiah	Persian official in Ammon, to the east of Judah. Part of an influential Jewish family, and most likely Jewish himself. Opposed Nehemiah.
Trans-Euphrates	Literally "beyond the river" (the Euphrates River). Refers to the whole area of Syria-Palestine, which was administered by a provincial governor or "satrap." Under him served local governors of Judah, Samaria, Ammon, etc.

SUGGESTED MEMORY
PASSAGES

And all the people gathered as one man into the square before the Water Gate. And they told Ezra the scribe to bring the Book of the Law of Moses that the LORD had commanded Israel. So Ezra the priest brought the Law before the assembly, both men and women and all who could understand what they heard, on the first day of the seventh month. And he read from it facing the square before the Water Gate from early morning until midday, in the presence of the men and the women and those who could understand. And the ears of all the people were attentive to the Book of the Law. (Neh. 8:1–3)

And Nehemiah, who was the governor, and Ezra the priest and scribe, and the Levites who taught the people said to all the people, "This day is holy to the LORD your God; do not mourn or weep." For all the people wept as they heard the words of the Law. Then he said to them, "Go your way. Eat the fat and drink sweet wine and send portions to anyone who has nothing ready, for this day is holy to our Lord. And do not be grieved, for the joy of the LORD is your strength." So the Levites calmed all the people, saying, "Be quiet, for this day is holy; do not be grieved." And all the people went their way to eat and drink and to send portions and to make great rejoicing, because they had understood the words that were declared to them. (Neh. 8:9–12)

Notes on Translations and Study Helps

This study can be done with any reliable translation of the Bible, although I do recommend the English Standard Version for its essentially literal but beautifully readable translation of the original languages.

These lessons can be completed with only the Bible open in front of you. The point is to grapple with the text, not with what others have said about the text. The goal is to know, increasingly, the joy and reward of digging into the Scriptures, God's breathed-out words which are not only able to make us wise for salvation through faith in Christ Jesus, but are also profitable for teaching, reproof, correction, and training in righteousness, that each of us may be competent, equipped for every good work (2 Tim. 3:15–17). To help you "dig in," basic and helpful contexts and comments are given throughout the lessons. I have used and learned from the following books in my own study and preparation; you may find sources such as these helpful at some point.

General Handbooks:

The Crossway Comprehensive Concordance of the Holy Bible: English Standard Version. Compiled by William D. Mounce. Wheaton, IL: Crossway Books, 2002. (Other concordances are available from various publishers and for different translations.)

The Illustrated Bible Dictionary. 4 vols. Wheaton: Tyndale House Publishers, 1980. (*The Zondervan Pictorial Encyclopedia of the Bible* is similarly helpful.)

Ryken, Leland, Philip Ryken, and James Wilhoit. *Ryken's Bible Handbook.* Wheaton: Tyndale House Publishers, 2005.

Vine's Complete Expository Dictionary of Old and New Testament Words. Nashville: Thomas Nelson Inc., 1984.

COMMENTARIES:

Dever, Mark. *The Message of the Old Testament.* Wheaton: Crossway Books, 2006.

Kidner, Derek. *Ezra and Nehemiah.* Tyndale Old Testament Commentary Series. Leicester, England: Inter-Varsity Press, 1979.

McConville, J. G. *Ezra, Nehemiah, and Esther.* The Daily Bible Study Series. Philadelphia: The Westminster Press, 1985.

Packer, J. I. *A Passion for Faithfulness: Wisdom from the Book of Nehemiah.* Wheaton: Crossway Books, 1995.

STUDY BIBLE:

ESV Study Bible. English Standard Version. Wheaton, IL: Crossway Bibles, 2008.

A native of St. Louis, Missouri, **Kathleen Nielson** holds M.A. and Ph.D. degrees in literature from Vanderbilt University and a B.A. from Wheaton College (Illinois). She has taught in the English departments at Vanderbilt University, Bethel College (Minnesota), and Wheaton College. She is the author of numerous Bible studies, as well as various articles and poems. Kathleen has directed and taught women's Bible studies at several churches and speaks extensively at conferences and retreats. Kathleen is married to Dr. Niel Nielson, president of Covenant College in Lookout Mountain, Georgia. Kathleen and Niel have three sons and two beautiful daughters-in-law.